CLIFFHANGER WRITING PROMPTS

30 One-Page Story Starters That Fire Up Kids' Imaginations and Help Them Develop Strong Narrative Writing Skills

Teresa Klepinger

New York • Toronto • London • Auckland • Sydney
Mexico City • New Delhi • Hong Kong • Buenos Aires

Teaching *Resources*

Dedication

To Lauren and her sleepover friends,
whose late-night storytelling inspired this book.
And with thanks to my family and writer friends
who supported me every step of the way.

Editor: Mela Ottaiano
Cover design: Jason Robinson
Interior design: Keka Interactive
Cover and interior illustrations: Alan@kja-artists.com

ISBN: 978-0-545-31511-1

Contents

Introduction

TURN THE IMAGINATION LOOSE!

Give a group of kids the chance to stretch their imagination muscles, and you'll find yourself listening to stories about the hip-hop-dancing, alien ants they found in the backyard, or the giant chocolate chip cookie singing the national anthem under the floor of the barn. In my visits to schools to give my "And Then . . ." storytelling presentations, I've heard kids of all ages tell some delightfully jaw-dropping whoppers. Whether students are polishing their storytelling skills in front of a group, or writing madly at a desk, I'm consistently impressed with their ability to take stories in directions that never would occur to my adult brain.

Each writing prompt in this book takes the form of a "cliffhanger" story-starter—exciting, maybe a little scary, and most certainly silly—that builds to a climax and is left unfinished. When the story gets to "And then . . ." at the end of the page, it's up to your students to decide how the story continues. The purpose of this book is to get students' imaginations fired up and their creative juices flowing. Once they realize that there are no "right" answers to what happens next, their brainstorming becomes boundless. Moreover, these stories can be used again and again, and they never turn out the same way twice.

When it comes to creative writing, many students find that the hardest part is getting started: "Write a story? About what?" These cliffhangers are designed to get students past that initial writer's block by providing helpful scaffolding such as

Reluctant Writers?

Students experience success with this approach from early elementary through middle school. Even the most resistant writers benefit. A teacher once commented to me about one of her students, "He has written more for you in five minutes than he did during his entire state assessment!"

characters, a setting, and a beginning plotline. So much of students' writing is tightly controlled—with measured outcomes, predetermined vocabulary, and required structures—that it may take them time to realize that when it comes to finishing these stories, anything goes! The difference between ordinary creative writing work and the work they'll do using these stories is like the difference between a P.E. class and a joyful romp on a playground where kids learn motor skills without being aware that learning is taking place. And Then . . . is the playground where learning happens.

Scheduling your time.

You can take students through these introductory steps in one session of 45 minutes to an hour; however, depending on the needs and abilities of your students, you may want to do the work over the course of a few days.

HOW TO USE THIS BOOK

Follow the step-by-step process to help students unlock their imaginations.

Step 1: Introducing the Stories

Choose four outgoing students to stand with you at the front of the room. Tell them you're going to read the beginning of a story, and when you come to the part that says "And then . . .," the first student will have exactly one minute to continue the story. When the minute is up, the second student will have exactly one minute to add to the story continuing from where the first student left off. When that minute is up, the third student must keep the story going for one minute. Finally, the last student has one minute more to end the story however he or she wants it to end. During a presentation, I simply watch the second hand on a clock or on my watch to keep time. A ticking timer can be too distracting.

A good writer is a good listener.

It is important for the rest of the class to listen quietly so student storytellers can come up with their own ideas when it is their turn. Good storytellers and writers are also inspired by others, so remind students to listen attentively whenever peers are sharing their writing with the class.

Select a story and read it aloud until you reach the place where the students will continue with the story. In a slightly exaggerated tone, say "And then . . .," and ask the first student to tell what happens next. When the first minute is up, prompt the next student, and continue until all four have had a turn and the story is completed. Give a round of applause to the group when the story is finished.

Your introduction to the activity should be lighthearted, so students understand that there is no "right" way to continue the story, and that the bigger the imagination, the bigger the fun.

Step 2: Group Storytelling

Divide the class into groups of four to six. The students in each group should be sitting in close proximity to each other.

Tell them you will read another story aloud, only this time when you read "And then . . ." each member of the group is going to add just one sentence to the story to tell what happens next. Have students choose who will go first, second, third, and so on. After the first student has added a sentence, the second student will build on that and add the next sentence until each student has a turn. Allow several minutes so students have time to complete the story. Give a signal to remind the last student to end the story—in just one sentence!

When you have read the story and started students on their journey, circulate around the room listening in and keeping the groups on track, making sure fellow classmates are waiting their turn and are not trying to push others to take the story in a particular direction.

The group dynamic!

When students are working in a group, and especially when they are working on these stories, they will often try to outdo one another when it comes to being funny, gross, or outrageous. While you do need to maintain classroom control, you should encourage them to be imaginative and creative. As long as students are being collaborative and productive (and not too loud), just let them be.

We all love a good story.

I have found the students love to hear each others' stories. It's also fun to collect them for a class book they can read during free reading time. (See "Create a Class Book or Stage a Storytelling Event," page 12.)

Choose a group that you noticed had a particularly imaginative storyline going and ask someone from that group to share what happened in their version of the story. Applaud the group and ask if another group wants to share. Give the class a few minutes to enjoy listening to each other.

One of the major benefits of this oral exercise is that students don't have to commit their ideas to paper yet, alleviating any of that type of pressure that may give rise to writer's block.

Step 3: Writing

Now that the class understands the process, the last step is for each student to write a personal ending to a story. Inform them that you will read one more story aloud, and this time they will write what happens next completely on their own. To keep each individual's ideas unique, it is vital that no one talks before they begin writing.

With paper and pencils ready, choose another story and read it aloud. Remind students to work silently, and let them begin. Give the class five to ten minutes to write, or more if they ask for it and your schedule allows for it. When the time is up, ask for volunteers to read aloud their results. Praise their efforts and applaud their imaginations.

Once your students have worked on a few of these fantastic tales, they will be experts at them, and probably pretty eager to write more. It's a great way to get even the most reluctant students to think of themselves as writers! And best of all, students can use their own work during language arts lessons that explore revision strategies and writing conventions; character, setting, and plot development; the writing traits; or whatever

> *Success for all is fun for all.*
>
> It is important to make sure your ELL students and struggling readers and writers can succeed. Offer them support in these activities. It is particularly helpful to those who are struggling with reading to hear a story-starter read aloud. This frees their minds and their time for getting ideas down on paper. During the writing process, offer extra support as needed to ELL students or partner them with helpful students.

you may be focusing on in your writing curriculum. And Then . . . stories will result in rich material that your students are excited about. With 30 stories, you can offer them creative writing assignments week after week—and they'll definitely come back asking for more!

Step 4: Working Independently

Follow up by providing a story-starter for students to read and complete on their own either in class or at home. After the practice you've already had together as a group, they will be more able to write and less likely to get stuck. Encourage students to write a minimum of one page, and a maximum five pages.

> *A question is often the answer.*
>
> If a student has trouble coming up with something, without giving suggestions or directions, ask very simple questions, such as, "What happened when he opened the door?"

TIPS FOR THE WRITING PROCESS

Photocopy and Distribute the Prompts

While you may choose to read aloud the stories exclusively, recalling the oral storytelling tradition, many students, especially ELLs, will benefit from having a copy of the story starter handy when it comes time to write. Distribute the copies either before or after you have read the story aloud, depending

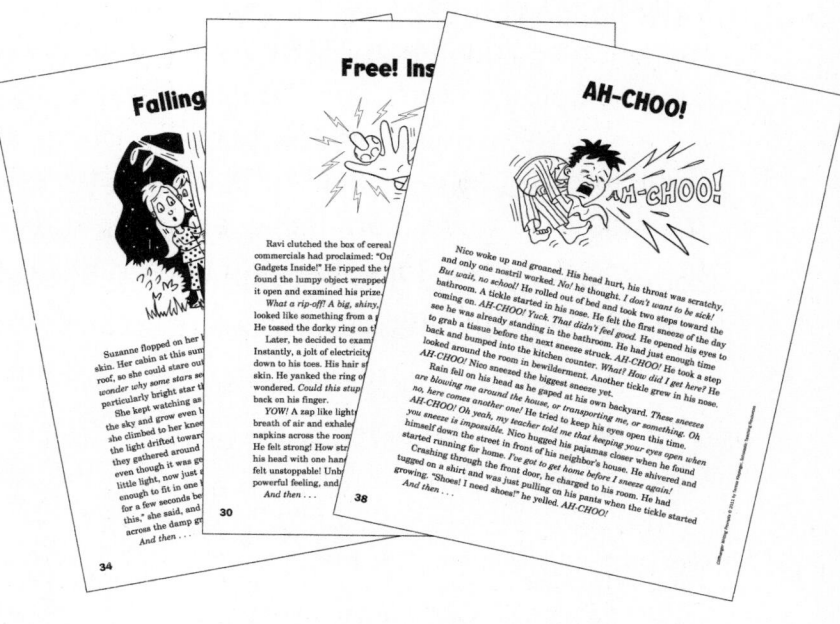

on the needs of your class. If you plan on putting together a class collection of these stories, it is also important to include the story-starter page together with students' continuations. Students may also enjoy writing the final versions of their stories on special stationery. Copy and have handy a supply of the stationery sheets on pages 19 and 20, or let students create their own stationery with decorative borders.

Teach Transition Words and Phrases

Students will tend to expand their storytelling time by creating run-on sentences using one "and then" after another. On a separate day, consider offering a quick mini-lesson, as needed, to show students how to avoid doing this by using transition words and phrases. You can also photocopy the "Transition Words and Phrases" reproducible (page 16) for students, and go over the list with them. Encourage students to keep the list in a Writer's Notebook, Language Arts folder, or writing journal to use as a reference when they are writing.

Encourage the Use of Interesting and Expressive Words

A rich vocabulary is key if students are to become successful readers and writers. Exploring synonyms and other alternatives for boring, overused words (such as *said*, *nice*, and *good*) will help your students build a better vocabulary and become better writers. Specific instruction in individual words and word-learning strategies is an important part of any language arts curriculum. One of the most successful ways to provide this kind of instruction is also the most fun for your students. Let students brainstorm their own wonderful word choices. Here's how:

Before introducing a story-starter, you might engage students in a quick, easy, vocabulary-brainstorming activity for words that relate to that story's theme. For example, if you're going to be using "Something's Fishy" (page 55), have students brainstorm words related to fish, water, and swimming; if you're working on "Better Run Fast!" (page 27), have students come up with words related to dinosaurs, amusement parks, running, and being scared. From time to time, it is always a great idea to do a quick vocabulary-enhancing activity to remind students to avoid mundane words like, *scary*, *funny*, *big*, *little*, and so on.

When brainstorming, consider using the "My Own List of Interesting and Expressive Words" reproducible on page 15. Students can brainstorm as part of a whole-class mini-lesson, as a small-group or partner activity, or even as homework or independent work when revising their writing. If a student has used the all-too-common word *great*, for example, under the "I can try" header on the reproducible, he or she can write *fantastic*, *fabulous*, *remarkable*, *stupendous*, or lots of other words to try. You can make multiple photocopies and keep them on hand in a writing center for students to use as needed for any writing activities. Encourage students to keep a copy of these lists in their Writer's Notebook, Language Arts folder, or writing journal to use as a reference when they are writing and revising.

Make Time for Peer Review and for Editing

Although the And Then . . . activities are intended to foster spontaneous creativity and enjoyment of the writing process, the resulting stories are great material for several aspects of your broader language arts curriculum, such as editing and revising for word choice, tone and voice, sentence fluency, and interest; as well as for proofreading for grammar, punctuation, and spelling. These will be particularly important if you are planning to "publish" a class collection of And Then . . . stories. Note: If your curriculum does not already call for specific lessons on grammar and usage, punctuation and mechanics (especially writing dialogue and using quotation marks), and other writing conventions (related topics such as tone, voice, and fluency), consider offering mini-lessons from time to time, as needed, to the whole-class or groups of students.

Once students have completed drafts of their stories, you might have them each work with a partner on a different day to read and review each other's work. First, photocopy and distribute to each student a copy of the "And Then . . . Peer Review Sheet" on page 17. Before partners begin the peer review, take a few minutes to go over the sheet with the class to make sure they understand what is expected.

After the peer review is finished, students can use that information to create a final draft. This activity can also be incorporated into a curriculum that features specific instruction in writing mechanics, writing traits, and editing, and can be done as Writing Center work, independent work, or as homework. Before students write out their final versions, provide them each with a copy of the "Editing and Revision Checklist" (page 18). Ask students to use their best penmanship to write out their conclusions to the stories on the special stationery sheets or on stationery they have created.

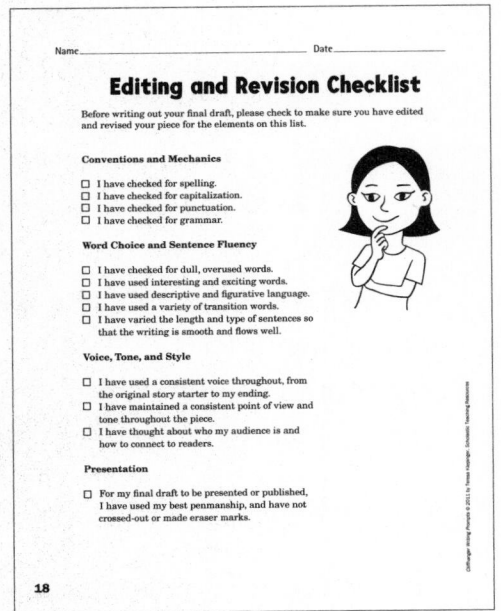

Create a Class Book or Stage a Storytelling Event

After students have completed several stories, let each student select his or her favorite to put in a class book. To make the class book, organize chapters according to the different story starters. Place a specific story starter at the beginning of a section and arrange all the student continuations of that story after that initial page. There may be more than one version of each story. Next, have students collaborate on a cover design. Bind together all the pages, and place the book in the classroom library or Reading Center.

You might also consider holding a storytelling event by staging a reading of the stories. Have each student choose his or her own personal favorite. Make sure each student has the appropriate story-starter page! Allow students time, in class or at home, to practice reading their stories. Set a date for the reading and invite students' families or other classes to attend.

Student
Activity Pages

My Own List of
Interesting and Expressive Words

For _____
I can try:

_____

_____

_____

For _____
I can try:

_____

_____

_____

For _____
I can try:

_____

_____

_____

For _____
I can try:

_____

_____

_____

For _____
I can try:

_____

_____

_____

For _____
I can try:

_____

_____

_____

For _____
I can try:

_____

_____

_____

For _____
I can try:

_____

_____

_____

For _____
I can try:

_____

_____

_____

For _____
I can try:

_____

_____

For _____
I can try:

_____

_____

For _____
I can try:

_____

_____

Name_____ Date_____

Transition Words and Phrases

Transition words help move the story along, from one sentence to the next and from one paragraph to the next. Here's a list of transition words and phrases you can refer to when you are writing.

Story Starters

- This morning
- Yesterday
- Today
- Last night (week, year, summer, winter, etc.)
- One day
- When I was (a baby, six years old, etc.)
- At camp
- It started when
- I remember when

Ordering Events

- Then
- Next
- Suddenly
- After that
- Soon after
- Eventually
- Later
- First
- Secondly
- Shortly thereafter
- Meanwhile

Story Enders

- Finally
- At last
- In the end
- When we were done
- At the end of (the day, night, visit, etc.)
- Last of all
- Ultimately
- In conclusion
- The upshot was
- To sum up

Other Transitional Words and Phrases

At the beginning
In the meantime
Lastly
First
While
In short
Second
When
The best part

Third
Another
The most important
Initially
Following this
The worst
Soon
We decided to
Another reason

When we finished
One time
Another time
Since then
At the same time
All at once
During
On the other hand
Besides

Use the lines below to jot down transitional words you come across in your own reading.

_____   _____   _____

_____   _____   _____

_____   _____   _____

_____   _____   _____

And Then . . .
Peer Review Sheet

Listen to your partner read his or her story, or read it for yourself, then answer the following questions. Circle your responses. Add any comments on the lines provided.

The story was: (You may circle more than one.)

Exciting	Surprising
Interesting	Gripping
Very funny	A little dull in some spots
Somewhat funny	Hard to follow
Scary	Inventive

Did the writer use interesting words?	Yes	No	Sometimes
Did the writer use action verbs?	Yes	No	Sometimes
Did the writer use powerful adjectives?	Yes	No	Sometimes
Did the writer vary the transition words?	Yes	No	Sometimes
Did the sentences flow smoothly?	Yes	No	Sometimes
Did the writer use correct grammar?	Yes	No	Mostly
Did the writer use a consistent style, tone, and voice from beginning to end?	Yes	No	Mostly
Did the ending work well?	Yes	No	Mostly

What did you like best about this story? What questions do you have? What could the writer do to improve the story?

_____

_____

_____

_____

_____

Editing and Revision Checklist

Before writing out your final draft, please check to make sure you have edited and revised your piece for the elements on this list.

Conventions and Mechanics

- ☐ I have checked for spelling.
- ☐ I have checked for capitalization.
- ☐ I have checked for punctuation.
- ☐ I have checked for grammar.

Word Choice and Sentence Fluency

- ☐ I have checked for dull, overused words.
- ☐ I have used interesting and exciting words.
- ☐ I have used descriptive and figurative language.
- ☐ I have used a variety of transition words.
- ☐ I have varied the length and type of sentences so that the writing is smooth and flows well.

Voice, Tone, and Style

- ☐ I have used a consistent voice throughout, from the original story starter to my ending.
- ☐ I have maintained a consistent point of view and tone throughout the piece.
- ☐ I have thought about who my audience is and how to connect to readers.

Presentation

- ☐ For my final draft to be presented or published, I have used my best penmanship, and have not crossed-out or made eraser marks.

Cliffhanger Writing Prompts © 2011 by Teresa Klepinger, Scholastic Teaching Resources

Cliffhanger Writing Prompts

Door in the Floor

"Abandon hope, ye scalawag!" David yelled and swiped his stick sword at his friend Steven. They charged each other up and down the haystack in the old barn behind David's farmhouse. Today they were pirates, yesterday they were cowboys, tomorrow who knows?

"Arrrr! Blimey! You got me!" Steven uttered a dramatic gasp, clutched his chest and fell backward, down the stack of loose hay and onto the floor of the barn.

Laughing, David called, "Hey Steven, come on back up! You can stab me this time!" He called again, "Steven? Come on up." But Steven didn't appear.

"Hey David!" he heard Steven yell. "Come here! You gotta see this!"

"What? What'd you find?" David slid down the hay bales.

"Check this out. There's a door in the floor." Steven stood over what looked like a trap door. A large metal ring and two hinges were all that marked its place.

David frowned as he stood beside Steven. "That's really weird. I've never seen that before. Let's see where it goes." Together they grasped the ring and lifted with all their strength. A blast of hot wind hit their faces. Dust billowed around their feet. The scorching air smelled ancient and stale.

They let the trap door fall open with a thud and bent to look into the darkness.

And then . . .

Up, Up, and Away

Makenna walked across the soccer field toward the park swings, digging a pack of bubble gum out of her pocket. *I'll bet I can blow a REALLY big bubble if I chew the whole pack at once,* she thought. A few minutes later she crammed the last piece into her mouth.

As soon as the gum was soft enough, she positioned it just right and started to blow. One breath: It was as big as an apple. Two breaths: It was nearly as big as her head. Three breaths: *Wow! A new personal record!* She kept going. Four breaths. Five. Six!

Just then, a gust of wind blew through the park and tugged at her bubble. Makenna held on. She inhaled and blew again. It was enormous! Another stronger gust of wind took hold of it and pulled. Makenna clamped her lips on the gum. *No way! I won't give up on this bubble!* The wind pulled harder, lifting Makenna off her feet. She held on with her teeth as she swiftly rose up and up and up. Looking down, she saw the swing set, then the whole playing field next to it. How could she call for help with her teeth clenched on the bubble gum? All she could manage was a pathetic sound through her nose, "NNNNNNNNN!"

And then . . .

Differ from Writing Prompts © 2011 by Teresa Klepinger, Scholastic Teaching Resources

Push the Button

"How much longer, Dad?" asked Ryan from the back seat of the van.

"Just around the next corner and over the next hill," Dad replied with a tired voice.

"That's what you said last time, and the time before that," Stacie protested from the seat beside Ryan.

It was summer, and that meant a long drive to see Grandma and Grandpa. Boring, boring, boring. Ryan and Stacie had already complained, argued, and played a few rounds of the alphabet game and twenty questions. As they sat and tried to think of what to do next, Stacie said, "Ryan, what's that button next to your seat? I don't have one like it next to mine."

"A button? I don't have a button." He looked down at a round red button just below the armrest next to his seat. "Oh, that." In large white letters was the word "PUSH."

"How come I don't have one?" asked Stacie, looking around her seat.

"I dunno." Ryan shrugged. They both stared at it.

"Are you gonna push it?" Stacie looked at Ryan with wide eyes. "You better not."

Ryan looked at his sister, then down at the button. After a quick check to make sure Mom and Dad weren't looking, he reached his finger toward the red button. He pushed.

And then . . .

Voices in My Root Beer

The pizza parlor buzzed with the happy voices of Rachael's soccer team. They had won the last game of the season and were celebrating with a pizza party. Rachael and her teammates crowded into a booth, happily discussing their winning plays.

"I got drinks! Who wants root beer?" her coach asked, holding a pitcher in each hand.

"Right here! I do!" Rachael waved her arm. To her, there was absolutely no better drink in the world than root beer! Rachael loved the foam, the fizz, the spicy sweetness! She grabbed a pitcher and began filling her glass. The foam rose up immediately, and she waited for it to go down before topping it off. She leaned over to smell the lovely root beer smell. The bubbles popped and tickled her nose. But they didn't make a bubble-popping sound. She bent her ear next to the foam. What was she hearing? She closed her eyes and concentrated on the sound. Voices. She heard voices coming from the tiny bubbles! Yes, and she heard words, a little louder now. What were they saying? They were just loud enough to understand.

And then . . .

Cliffhanger Writing Prompts © 2011 by Teresa Klepinger Scholastic Teaching Resources

Better Run Fast!

Caleb scuffed his feet and kicked at a piece of garbage. This had to be the lamest amusement park ever. The place looked about a thousand years old and had mostly kiddie rides. There was one decent roller coaster and some bumper cars, but Caleb didn't see much else worth riding.

"Come on, Caleb," his mom called. "This next ride is going to be great!" She had that too-cheery voice she always used when she was trying to keep everyone jolly. It didn't fool him. He could tell she thought this was a pretty cheesy park, too. She held his two younger brothers' hands and smiled down at them. "Won't this be fun?" she called to Caleb and his dad, but she didn't wait for an answer.

They walked up to a building that looked like it was ready to fall over. It was pretty big, two stories, but no windows. "Land of the Dinosaurs" was painted on a peeling sign. Metal cars ran along a track that carried people through swinging doors and into the dark interior. *Oh, great*, Caleb thought as they all piled into a car. *There's probably a bunch of stupid mechanical dinosaurs that squeak when they move and blow smoke out of their nostrils. Maybe I can take a nap.* The car jolted forward through the flaps.

Colored lights illuminated palm trees, and volcanoes puffed steam a few feet from the jerky vehicle. They rounded a corner and came upon a big T-rex that was supposedly feeding on the carcass of a Triceratops.

It turned to face them as they approached. "This is the stupidest thing I've ever seen!" Caleb actually said aloud. But as they got closer, Caleb decided he might change his mind about this one. Its movements were pretty smooth, and the skin looked almost real. The T-rex swung its head closer to their car. *Wow! I can see its sides move like it's really breathing!*

Caleb's surprise quickly turned to shock, however, when he felt the dinosaur's hot breath blow in his face. The pupils of its eyes fixed on him, and a spray of spit hit him as it roared in fury.

And then . . .

Cliffhanger Writing Prompts © 2011 by Teresa Klepinger, Scholastic Teaching Resources

Pumpkin Surprise

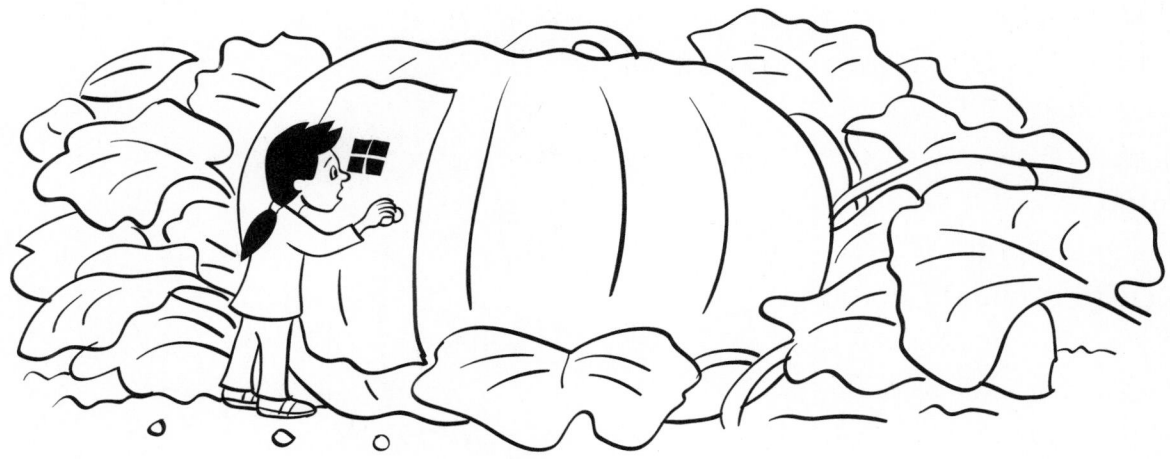

Stephanie knelt in the garden where she planned to grow her jack-o'-lantern. Tearing open the seed packet labeled "Pumpkin Surprise," she was surprised indeed. She saw only one tiny, shriveled seed. *Oh well*, she thought. *I hope it grows.* She dug a little hole, stuck the seed in, watered it, and went into the house.

The next morning on her way to the bus stop, Stephanie passed by the garden and couldn't believe what she saw. Her seed had already sprouted and had several leaves on a little vine! After school that afternoon, Stephanie's jaw dropped as she gazed at the pumpkin plant that she had just planted the day before. Its leaves were as big as dinner plates, and a tiny pumpkin rested on the soil. "Holy cow!" she breathed. "Pumpkin Surprise is right!"

The next day, Stephanie took one look at the garden and felt chills go down her spine. Her little pumpkin was now waist high and so wide she couldn't put her arms around it. How big was this thing going to get? She couldn't stop thinking about it the rest of the day.

As soon as she stepped off the bus, she dashed to the garden. From across the yard, she could see her enormous golden orange pumpkin towering above the other plants. Treading carefully, she stepped around it and stopped, startled. There was a door! It even had a little doorknob and a window to light the inside. Curious, she peeked in, twisted the handle, and pulled gently.

And then . . .

Free! Inside!

Ravi clutched the box of cereal he'd been waiting for. Finally! The commercials had proclaimed: "One of Five Real Working Superhero Gadgets Inside!" He ripped the top off, rummaged around inside, and found the lumpy object wrapped in several layers of packaging. He pulled it open and examined his prize.

What a rip-off! A big, shiny, plastic ring like a girl would wear! It looked like something from a gumball machine. *Some "Superhero Gadget."* He tossed the dorky ring on the counter and went to watch TV.

Later, he decided to examine it more closely and stuck it on his finger. Instantly, a jolt of electricity traveled up his arm, over his body, and down to his toes. His hair stood on end, and goosebumps raced across his skin. He yanked the ring off. The feeling went away. *What was that?* he wondered. *Could this stupid-looking ring be doing that?* Slowly, he slid it back on his finger.

YOW! A zap like lightning burned through his body. He gulped a deep breath of air and exhaled, blowing the cereal box and a whole stack of napkins across the room. What was happening? He flexed his muscles. He felt strong! How strong? Grabbing the kitchen chair, he hoisted it over his head with one hand. Ha! He took another breath. Such energy! He felt unstoppable! Unbreakable! Indestructible! He had to test this new, powerful feeling, and Ravi knew just what he was going to try first.

And then . . .

Cliffhanger Writing Prompts © 2011 by Teresa Klepinger, Scholastic Teaching Resources

Gone Camping

Brian lugged his sleeping bag and suitcase to the car, which was now stuffed to the roof with everything a family could possibly need for a weekend camping trip. He and his sister squeezed themselves into the back seat. Luckily, the drive was only an hour.

When they arrived at the entrance to the campground, the ranger at the gate took their money and pointed them toward the campsite. Just before they drove off he said, "By the way, we've heard reports of a strange animal around these parts. We don't quite know what it is, but I recommend keeping your children close after dark." Brian wasn't sure what that meant, but he didn't like the sound of it.

After helping his family set up, Brian was ready to go off exploring. There was still plenty of daylight left, so that "strange animal" wouldn't be bothering him, right?

"I'm going down to the creek, Mom," he called to his mother.

"I don't know about that, hon," his mom said. "You heard the park ranger."

"Oh Mom, I'll be fine. It's not far, and I'll stay on the path."

"All right, but be back in an hour," his mom relented.

Brian took off down the path into the forest. The woods had great trees to climb and the nearby creek had a cool wading spot. Later, on his way back up the trail to camp, he heard a rustling in the bushes. He froze, remembering the warning from the park ranger. He was about to make a run for it, but he stopped. Just one little peek wouldn't hurt, would it? Quietly, he tiptoed over to the spot where he saw the leaves quivering. *Aw, it can't be very big,* he thought. He crouched and reached out to spread the branches apart. Squinting into the center of the underbrush, he found himself face to face with the creature.

"You're not going to hurt me, are you?" it asked.

And then . . .

Cliffhanger Writing Prompts © 2011 by Teresa Klepinger, Scholastic Teaching Resources

Cookie UFO

Jasmine dropped her lunch box on the cafeteria table and sat down next to Casey.

"Did you hear?" Jasmine said. "It's some first grader's birthday and his mom brought cookies for *everyone*!"

"Everyone? Awesome!" Casey replied.

As they finished their lunches, the cafeteria workers walked past the tables, setting plates of cookies in front of eager students. "One each," the stern ladies reminded everyone.

"What kind of cookies are those?" Casey asked, peering down at the plate. "They're sorta weird looking."

They stared at the cookies. Normal sugar cookies have little sugar crystals sprinkled on top. These had crystals, but they sure weren't normal. They sparkled and glowed and gave off light like little stars. A faint buzzing noise started, then quickly grew louder. Other kids stopped talking and stared as the cookies trembled, then rose from the table and began to spin.

"Jasmine, what are they doing?" Casey squeaked.

A girl squealed. Someone else yelled "Hey, look!" The cookies spun faster and faster. Colored lights flashed as they began to float around the cafeteria. The lunch lady blew her whistle and ordered everyone out to the playground, but Jasmine and Casey stayed, waiting to see what would happen next.

And then . . .

Cliffhanger Writing Prompts © 2011 by Teresa Klepinger, Scholastic Teaching Resources

Falling Star

Suzanne flopped on her bunk, her nightgown sticking to her sweaty skin. Her cabin at this summer camp only had wooden floors and a fabric roof, so she could stare out at the stars glittering in the clear sky. *I wonder why some stars seem to twinkle,* she thought as she watched one particularly bright star that glimmered more than the others.

She kept watching as it seemed not only to twinkle, but to glide across the sky and grow even brighter. "Hey everyone, look at that!" she said, as she climbed to her knees. "That star is moving!" She stared in surprise as the light drifted towards her cabin site. Several girls jumped on her bed as they gathered around to watch. "Is it a spaceship?" someone asked. But no, even though it was getting nearer, it really wasn't very big. In fact, this little light, now just above the treetops, was kind of tiny. It seemed small enough to fit in one hand. They heard it humming a low note as it hovered for a few seconds before slowly descending to the ground. "I've got to see this," she said, and the whole gang followed her down the steps. Tiptoeing across the damp grass, they slowly approached the shining object.

And then . . .

Cliffhanger Writing Prompts © 2011 by Teresa Klepinger, Scholastic Teaching Resources

Special Delivery

Ding dong. Sallie heard the doorbell ring, then her mom opening the door. She mumbled something and then called, "Hey Sallie, you've got a package from your wacky uncle!"

In a flash, Sallie was on her way. Her birthday was in three days, and this had to be her present from Uncle Russ. This amazingly cool guy traveled all over the world to exotic places, and every year he sent Sallie a birthday present that somehow surpassed the one she got the year before.

Sallie skidded to a stop in front of her mom who held a huge square box. Taking it in her arms, Sallie was shocked at how light it was. It felt empty! But she knew whatever was inside would be something incredibly awesome and wonderfully weird. She quickly sliced through the packing tape with scissors, opened the flaps, and started digging through armfuls of foam bits. The first thing she came across was an envelope. Opening it, she read:

> Dearest Sallie,
>
> Happy Birthday! I found this in a tiny shop hidden away in a village on an island in the Indian Ocean. At first I wasn't sure about giving it to someone as young as you, but I think you can handle it. I just hope I don't get in trouble with your mother. Enjoy! But be careful.
>
> Love,
> Uncle Russ

Sallie tossed the note aside and dug through the box again. She found a perfectly round sphere the size of a soccer ball. It was made of dark smooth wood, but felt almost weightless. A seam went around the middle, a gold hinge held the two halves together, and an ornate clasp latched it shut.

Sallie sat back. *What in the world* is *this?* she thought. She twisted the clasp and released the latch. It sprang open.

And then . . .

Cliffhanger Writing Prompts © 2011 by Teresa Klepinger, Scholastic Teaching Resources

Flower Power

"Sara, come see this!" Lauren called to her big sister as they walked home from school.

"Oh, come on, Lauren. You're such a slowpoke."

"I'm not a slowpoke. Look at these flowers!"

"We've seen these flowers a million times," Sara complained. "And I want to get home. I'm hungry."

"These are different. Really different. Look." Lauren squatted beside a patch of bright orange flowers.

Sighing, Sara started back. "What's so special about a bunch of orange . . . What's that noise?" A sound of bells, or tinkling glass, grew louder with each step. "That's not the flowers, is it?"

"Yeah, it is. You can smell them, too." Lauren took a deep breath. Her sister did the same and inhaled a scent like chocolate, honey, and cotton candy all at once.

Each tightly closed bloom was about the size of a fist perched on the end of a long stem, but they didn't face the sun the way most flowers do. One flower stood straight in the center of the patch, while the others bobbed their heads toward it, like subjects before a throne.

"What are they doing?" Lauren asked.

"I think they're bowing to the middle flower," Sara answered, and as they watched, a light began shining from inside the center flower, quivering like a little flame. The girls' eyes grew wide as the petals slowly began to open, first the outer petals, then an inner layer. Finally, the flower fully opened, and the girls witnessed what no eye had seen before.

And then . . .

AH-CHOO!

Nico woke up and groaned. His head hurt, his throat was scratchy, and only one nostril worked. *No!* he thought. *I don't want to be sick! But wait, no school!* He rolled out of bed and took two steps toward the bathroom. A tickle started in his nose. He felt the first sneeze of the day coming on. *AH-CHOO! Yuck. That didn't feel good.* He opened his eyes to see he was already standing in the bathroom. He had just enough time to grab a tissue before the next sneeze struck. *AH-CHOO!* He took a step back and bumped into the kitchen counter. *What? How did I get here?* He looked around the room in bewilderment. Another tickle grew in his nose. *AH-CHOO!* Nico sneezed the biggest sneeze yet.

Rain fell on his head as he gaped at his own backyard. *These sneezes are blowing me around the house, or transporting me, or something. Oh no, here comes another one!* He tried to keep his eyes open this time. *AH-CHOO! Oh yeah, my teacher told me that keeping your eyes open when you sneeze is impossible.* Nico hugged his pajamas closer when he found himself down the street in front of his neighbor's house. He shivered and started running for home. *I've got to get home before I sneeze again!*

Crashing through the front door, he charged to his room. He had tugged on a shirt and was just pulling on his pants when the tickle started growing. "Shoes! I need shoes!" he yelled. *AH-CHOO!*

And then . . .

Cliffhanger Writing Prompts © 2011 by Teresa Klepinger, Scholastic Teaching Resources

Genie in My Lamp

Maria couldn't wait to plug in the new, adorable, pink lamp she got for her birthday. It had a round base in an eye-popping shade of hot pink, which she loved. But the best part was the lampshade. It was white with shiny pink polka dots, a row of pink puffballs around the top, and a swishy pink fringe that hung off the bottom edge. It even had twinkle lights that sparkled from inside the shade.

Maria put the lamp on her desk and plugged it in. The lamp trembled. Purple smoke poured from the top. Maria jumped on her bed, watching in amazement. The smoke slowly formed into the upper part of a man. He had dark skin and wore a turban, though where his legs should be, he had only the lamp shade.

"I AM THE GENIE OF THE LAMP," he spoke grandly.

Maria couldn't help smiling. The Genie of the Lamp was wearing her polka-dotted, sparkly lampshade like a skirt. She giggled. He really looked ridiculous.

"Why are you amused?" asked the genie, his expression stern. When he spoke, his lampshade skirt swished smartly.

"I'm sorry, but you do look kind of funny wearing my lampshade."

The genie looked down at the lamp. "Ah, I see," he said. He sighed. "I had some trouble with the International Genie Association last week.

Cliffhanger Writing Prompts © 2011 by Teresa Klepinger, Scholastic Teaching Resources

Obviously, this is their idea of a punishment. Nevertheless, we must proceed." He cleared his throat and spoke grandly again. "YOU ARE MY MASTER. YOUR WISH IS MY COMMAND."

"My wish? You'll really grant me a wish?" Maria asked.

The genie rolled his eyes a little. "Of course," he said. "The one who calls me from my lamp is granted a wish."

"That's great! I've always known what I would do if I could have a wish granted. Genie, I wish for one thousand wishes." Maria thought this was pretty clever.

"I'm sorry. That is not allowed. International Genie Association rule 437(a): The wisher cannot wish for more wishes."

"Well then, I wish for all the money I could ever want." Maria imagined a stable of horses, a huge house, a limo with her own driver.

"That is not possible either. Rule 437(b) states that no genie may grant an unlimited supply of anything to the wisher."

"What? I never knew genies came with all these rules! All right, let me think." Maria pondered for a moment. "I've got it, Genie. This is perfect." She took a deep breath, closed her eyes, and spoke her wish. The genie smiled.

And then . . .

Cliffhanger Writing Prompts © 2011 by Teresa Klepinger, Scholastic Teaching Resources

Ants in Your Pants

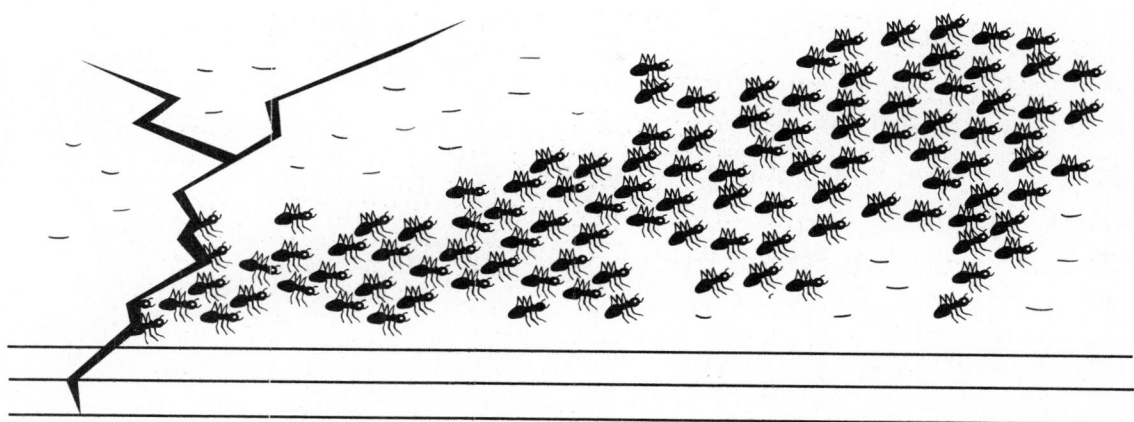

Winston sat on the curb and scratched a stick on the cement while he waited for his friend. A car approached, and he looked up, but it passed by. He poked his stick into the crack where some weeds were growing. Several ants came dashing out of the crevice. He stabbed his stick at them, trying to crush one, but they were too fast for him. More ants poured out of the crack, and Winston stood up before they could crawl into his shorts.

Finally, a car pulled up to the curb. "Marcus! I thought you'd never get here!" Winston exclaimed. Marcus climbed out of the car, waved to his grandma, and the car moved on.

"What's with the stick?" Marcus asked.

"Just poking an ant hill. You'd better move over or they're going to climb all over your shoes."

Marcus stepped back and looked down. Hundreds of ants were gushing onto the sidewalk. The two boys watched as the ants scurried this way and that.

"What do you think they're trying to do?" Winston asked.

Marcus shrugged. "Protect the ant hill, I guess."

"From us? Fat chance. I could squish fifty of them at a time." Winston kept watching as the ants began to gather in groups, forming several masses of ant bodies across the squares of cement. Then each heap began to shape itself, rolling and rippling until a definite form took place.

Winston and Marcus stared in wonder as they read what the ants had spelled.

And then . . .

Still Life

Clifton's art teacher must have been having a good day. He was letting the students draw anything they wanted, so Clifton started in on his favorite subject, horses. He outlined a horse with his marker, adding a cowboy next to it. Then he began coloring them in with crayon, dark brown for the horse's body, black for its mane and tail. The cowboy got blue jeans, brown boots, and a red shirt.

Just as he started coloring the landscape, the horse shook its mane and snorted. Clifton gasped, dropping his crayons. The cowboy turned his head to look at the boy.

"Well howdy there, young fella," he said. "Mighty nice drawin' ya done here. Ah, 'scuse me while I catch my horse 'fore he gits away."

Clifton watched wide-eyed as the horse wandered to the edge of the paper, sniffing the white ground. The cowboy turned again to Clifton.

"Got a bit of a problem here," he said. "Looks like you forgot to draw in his bridle, so I got nothin' to grab hold of. Would ya mind drawin' it in? I gotta catch my horse."

Clifton grabbed his marker and colored in a bridle and reins.

"Mighty kind of ya," the cowboy said, and reached for his horse. But the horse tossed his head and turned towards the back of the picture. The cowboy lunged, and the horse broke into a trot.

"Where's my lasso? I need my lasso! Draw me one quick! My horse is gittin' away!"

And then . . .

Cliffhanger Writing Prompts © 2011 by Teresa Klepinger, Scholastic Teaching Resources

Family Outing

Christopher scuffed his feet along the trail as he followed his parents, three brothers, and sister through the woods. *I'm thirsty, my feet hurt, and I'm sure a million mosquitoes have bitten me by now*, he thought as he scratched at his elbow. "Will you guys slow down? Not everyone is feeling so energetic on this hike, you know." He scowled as his mom just turned and smiled at him. As his family's voices faded around a curve, he sat on a stump beside the path. *Well, I'm taking a rest even if they aren't.*

In the sudden quiet he became aware of odd sounds around him. Faint music, laughter, the clinking of glasses, and happy voices shouting to each other. *Sounds like a party*, he thought. *But how can there be a party in this wilderness?* Strangely, the noises seemed to originate in a clump of bushes just off the path. He stepped closer, quietly, hoping not to be seen spying. It was darker under the canopy of leaves, and what caught his eye was a beam of light shining straight out of a hole in the ground at the base of a tree. It was only as big as a rabbit hole, but the party noises were definitely coming from there. The music sounded like tiny fiddles, guitars, and horns.

Christopher tiptoed up to the hole and *snap!* He stepped on a dry twig. The noises ceased. Whispers took their place. Christopher crouched silently and waited.

And then . . .

Cliffhanger Writing Prompts © 2011 by Teresa Klepinger, Scholastic Teaching Resources

Swish

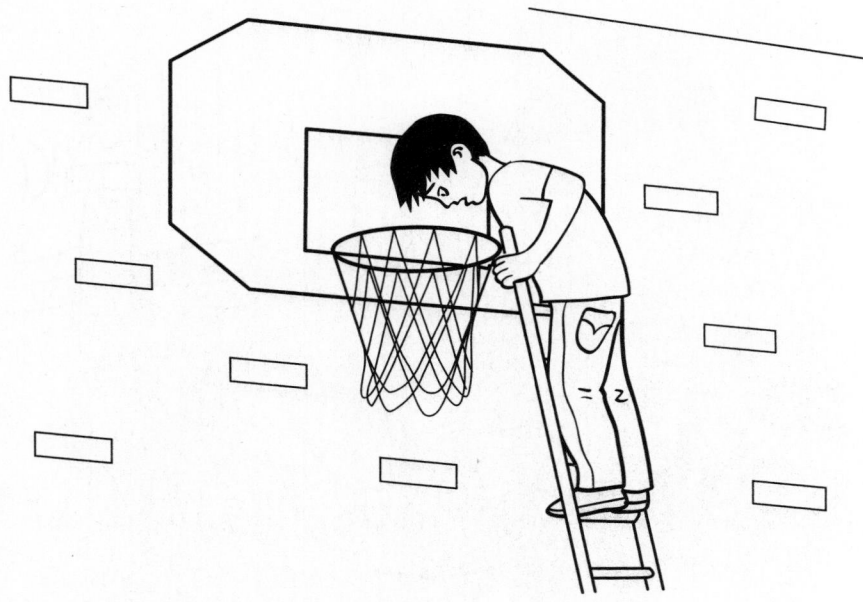

Kai grabbed his basketball from the floor of his closet and made his way out to the new hoop in the driveway. He dribbled a little to loosen up, then took his first shot. The ball bounced off the rim and into the bushes. *Whatever,* he thought. *I'm still warming up.* He circled the driveway, and charged the hoop, trying for a layup. *Drat!* Kai took a quick look up and down the street to make sure no neighborhood kids were watching him miss such easy shots. He bounced the ball three times, focused on the hoop, set his feet, and took the shot. The ball arced into the air and swished into the net.

Then silence. There was no bounce after the ball passed through the hoop. There was no ball. It was gone. Kai looked around him. How could he have missed it? He backed up and looked up on the roof. No ball. How could the ball disappear when it just went through the net?

On impulse, Kai picked up a rock and tossed it into the hoop. No rock came out the bottom. It vanished. Kai shivered. *Okay, I must be going crazy. What is going on here?* He stood there for a moment, then opened the garage door and dragged out the ladder, unfolding it next to the hoop. He slowly climbed the rungs. When he reached the top, he looked down into the basket.

And then . . .

Cliffhanger Writing Prompts © 2011 by Teresa Klepinger, Scholastic Teaching Resources

Sand Castle

Mason dumped his stuff on the damp sand, the kind that's perfect for building a castle. After a week at this place, he was getting pretty good. The tide was going out, so he knew he had several hours before the waves would flood his site. *Hope Mom doesn't notice all the stuff I swiped from the kitchen*, he thought, as he emptied a bag of tools.

After an hour of steady effort, he sat back and viewed his creation. *Hmmm, still has a ways to go. The moat is good, and the walls are smooth, but it's still too plain.* His stomach growled. *I'll add the details after lunch.* He hiked back up the sand dune to the beach house, collecting bits of stuff along the way—feathers, shells, small seaweed leaves.

Mason wolfed down his mac and cheese and slid back down the dune, anxious to get back to work. *Someone's been messing with my castle!* he thought as he approached it. He scanned the beach in both directions, but it was deserted. He squatted to get a better look at the damage. *Actually, it's not really ruined, but it's definitely different.* He saw tiny flags flying from the towers. Turrets had been carved around the top. An actual wooden drawbridge with miniature chains blocked the castle door

Cliffhanger Writing Prompts © 2011 by Teresa Klepinger, Scholastic Teaching Resources

facing the moat. The moat itself was filled with water, which Mason never seemed able to accomplish. *Whoa! There's something swimming in it! At first glance, he thought it was a salamander, but when he looked more closely, he saw scales and a mouth full of sharp teeth. No way! That's a real alligator!*

Mason flattened himself on his stomach in the sand. He could see faint carvings in the sand walls that made it look like stone. There 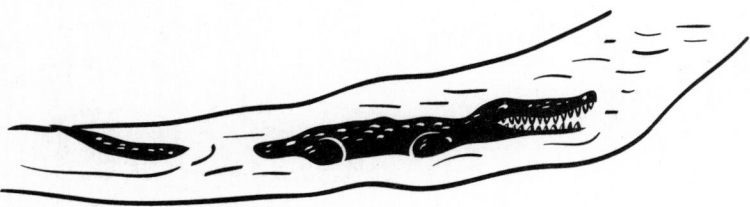 were window openings that seemed to disappear into darkness. But his skin tingled when the drawbridge began to descend. He could hear the tiny chains clanking and the wood creaking as it slowly lowered across the moat.

And then . . .

Take a Deep Breath

The ocean waves pounded the sand and slithered up to Cameryn's feet. She bounded into the surf, each leap bringing the water deeper, to her knees, to her thighs, to her hips. Finally another breaker knocked her off her feet. She fell, laughing, and enjoyed the coolness of the water on her hot skin. Just as her feet found the sand again another wave crashed on her head and hammered her below the surface. She barely had time to grab a breath before the water closed over her. She tumbled and rolled beneath the waves. Which way was up? She was running out of air. Finally, she couldn't hold her breath any longer, and her lungs sucked in the seawater.

But she didn't choke. She didn't feel faint. Her head cleared, and she opened her eyes. She saw the sand beneath her, and the legs of other swimmers kicking below the surface. She exhaled the water from her lungs, and automatically sucked in another breath. It didn't hurt. In fact, she felt fine, perfectly fine. *I'm breathing underwater! This is so weird!* She swam a little farther out, past the waves that were breaking above her, to where the water was calm and the sea floor dropped away. Cameryn could see schools of fish, rock formations, even what looked like a long-buried object sticking out of the sand. *I could stay down here for hours,* she thought, as she spotted something huge in the distance.

And then . . .

Going Up

Daniel wasn't really thrilled about the new apartment building his family had moved into. The only cool thing about it was the elevator. His old building didn't have one, but now they lived on the fourth floor, so he got to ride it every day.

Today he was going home and was about to turn right to his hall elevator when he decided to mix things up and turn left instead. There was an elevator for this hall, too, so why not give it a try? He pushed the up arrow and stepped in. *Good! No one else going up.* He reached for button number four but was suddenly confused by the panel. There were lots more than four numbers. In fact, the numbers went all the way to 36! *How can there be thirty-six numbers? There aren't thirty-six floors. Maybe it's a spare-parts elevator, and only the first four buttons work.* But since he was in a mix-it-up mood, he decided to push a spare-part number. *Let's try number 29.* The number lit up, the doors closed, and the elevator started to rise. The display panel above the door read "2," then "3," then "4," and kept going. Daniel's heart started to pound. 15, 16, 17. His hands started to sweat. *How do I get out of here?* 22, 23, 24. The elevator slowed, then stopped when the panel read "29." The doors dinged and slid open.

"Hello, Daniel. Welcome to floor number 29."

And then . . .

Casting Spells

Nandita scanned the library shelves. There it was! She quickly checked out *Casting Spells* and shoved it in her backpack. This was the only book on wizards and magic she hadn't read, so she hoped it would be a good one. Of course, she knew it was all make-believe, but pretending was what made it all so much fun.

When she got home, Nandita opened the book to the table of contents. There were chapters called "Chants," "Incantations," "Love Spells," "Beauty Spells," and "Power Spells." Hmmm, which one to try first? "Power Spells" sounded good. She'd love to have power over her little sister, and Mom and Dad, too. Wouldn't it be cool to be the most powerful person in her school? Ha! *OBEY ME all you little people!*

She flipped to the page titled "Obedience Spell" and read the instructions. It seemed easy enough, so she set to work gathering materials: a candle (from the china closet), a purple cloth (from her sister's dress up box), a silver star (from a necklace), and a jewel (from her mother's jewelry box—*hope she doesn't mind*). She arranged everything as the book directed, read over the words a few times, then took a deep breath. Three times she spoke the magic words, just as instructed. Now what? Nothing seemed different. There was no cloud of smoke or flash of light. *Remember, it's only make believe.* Her mom poked her head in the door.

Cliffhanger Writing Prompts © 2011 by Teresa Klepinger, Scholastic Teaching Resources

"Time for dinner, Nandita."

At the dinner table, Mom put chicken on her plate, then started to spoon peas onto it. "Mom, don't give me peas!" she whined. Immediately her mom scooped the peas back into the bowl, every last one of them. Nandita looked up in surprise, but Mom's face was blank.

After dinner, Mom was washing dishes when Nandita came into the kitchen. "Let's play Monopoly tonight, Mom." Without a word, Mom put the pot she was scrubbing down in the sink, dried her hands, walked to the closet, and pulled out the Monopoly game. Nandita was shocked. She had expected her to say "after I finish the dishes," but she simply quit right then and there, again with that same blank face.

Nandita turned to her dad, who was watching TV. "Hey Dad, come play with us." Her father turned off the TV and walked to the table.

Oh my gosh, she realized. *They're obeying me. They're doing whatever I tell them to do.* She thought about that for a moment. A smile spread across her face. *This definitely has possibilities.*

And then . . .

Cliffhanger Writing Prompts © 2011 by Teresa Klepinger, Scholastic Teaching Resources

Disappearing Act

Derek clipped the leash on his dog and stepped out the front door. "Which way, Buddy?" The big mutt yanked him to the left, towards the trail that led to the park. "Whoa! Slow down! I'm coming! HEEL!" he yelled, lurching after his eager dog. He stumbled after him down the path and into the trees. As he passed the small meadow alongside the creek, he noticed something new. Someone had placed a large ring of rocks right in the middle of the grass. The ring was too big to be a campfire circle, and nothing looked burned in the middle. Derek stepped closer to get a better look.

Suddenly, Buddy charged forward, and the leash slipped from his hand. "Buddy! No! Come here!" Buddy wasn't listening as he crossed the meadow in three strides and leaped into the circle of rocks.

Then he disappeared.

"Buddy? Buddy!" Derek screamed.

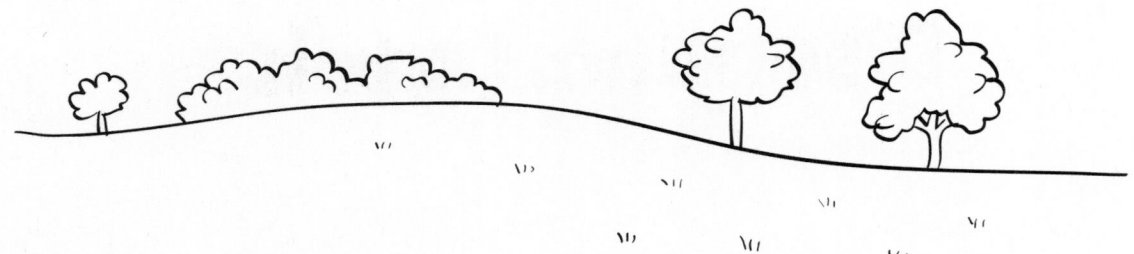

The next moment, Buddy was bounding out of the rock circle and happily banging his tail on Derek's legs. "Nutty dog, you scared me to death! What happened to you? Hey, what's that you've got?"

Derek reached for the object in Buddy's mouth. It was an ordinary stick. He turned it over in his hands, then tossed it aside. It bounced unexpectedly and flipped up and back into the circle of stones. Buddy took off after it. "Buddy no! Stay! NO!" he shouted after the dog. But Buddy again disappeared when he crossed the rock perimeter. Derek's heart thumped as he waited. One second, two seconds, three seconds. Out jumped the dog, his regular cheerful self. Derek grabbed the leash and wrapped it around his wrist. "Let's get out of here!" he said, then noticed Buddy had another object in his mouth. "What have you got this time, Buddy?" he asked, holding his hand out. Buddy obediently dropped it into his palm.

"Oh, ick!"

And then . . .

Cliffhanger Writing Prompts © 2011 by Teresa Klepinger, Scholastic Teaching Resources

Playing Catch

Brogan, Lizzie, and their dad plopped down on the picnic blanket spread on the grass in the sunny meadow. They all chewed their sandwiches and sipped drinks, watching the birds in the trees that ringed the grassy hillside.

When everyone had finished, Dad lay back, closed his eyes, and almost immediately began to snore.

"So what should we do now?" Lizzie asked.

"I dunno" her brother answered.

"Let's go climb trees."

"Betcha I'm in a tree before you!" Brogan answered, and he sprinted toward a likely looking tree with Lizzie racing close behind.

Brogan grabbed the lowest-hanging branch he came to and swung his legs up to cross his ankles over it. Lizzie found a foothold on the tree next to Brogan's, grasped a limb, and hoisted herself up. When Brogan was standing on his branch, Lizzie yelled, "Ha! I beat you!"

"No way!" he yelled back. "I got here first!"

"But I was standing in my tree first!"

"Yeah, but I . . ." Brogan stopped. "Whoa, Lizzie, what's going on?"

His tree began to sway. The branches around it waved as if a strong wind blew, even though the air was still. Lizzie shrieked as her tree bent and shivered, then began bouncing her up and down. She held on with all her might.

"Help!" Brogan shouted as a branch wrapped its twiggy fingers around his middle and plucked him off the limb. The tree waved him around in midair.

"Brogan!" Lizzie screamed as it tossed her brother, sending him sailing towards Lizzie's tree.

And then . . .

Cliffhanger Writing Prompts © 2011 by Teresa Klepinger, Scholastic Teaching Resources

Something's Fishy

The first thing Ava said when she arrived at her grandfather's summer lake house was, "Grandpa! Can I go swimming? I can really swim now. Can I? Will you come watch me?"

"Go swimming, huh? Well, I don't know," Grandpa responded hesitantly.

"What? Grandpa! I've really been looking forward to it!" Ava pleaded. "*Pleeease?*"

He coughed and looked uncomfortable. "Ava, that lake is . . . it might . . . I guess if I'm right there, but just tell me if you think . . . oh never mind! Sure, I'll come and watch you."

Next thing, Ava was galloping into the water while Grandpa sat in a lawn chair sipping a cold drink.

"Grandpa! Watch this!" She did a back somersault, and Grandpa smiled encouragingly. Then Ava dove deep, but instead of cool water down below, she felt warm water. *That's strange.* Coming up, she took a deep breath, and dove again. The water was definitely warm, almost like bath water,

Cliffhanger Writing Prompts © 2011 by Teresa Klepinger, Scholastic Teaching Resources

and it felt tingly on her skin. *What's going on?* As soon as she surfaced, she called out, "Grandpa! That was really strange. Just now when I dove down, the water was warm and made my skin feel all funny."

Grandpa sat straight up. "It did? Are you all right? You'd better come out of there. Did you see anything?"

"See anything? No. What do you mean?"

"Oh, good. I mean, let's head back to the house for lunch." As they walked back to the house, Grandpa kept looking at Ava and fussing over her, wrapping her towel more closely around her shoulders, smoothing her hair, patting her back.

"You feel OK?" he asked.

"Yeah, why?" Grandpa said nothing.

While Grandpa fixed sandwiches, Ava showered to try to wash off that tingly feeling that wouldn't go away. Standing in the spray, she scrubbed her arms with the bar of soap. Her skin felt scratchy. Something wasn't right. She looked down at her arms and was horrified to see what looked like scales.

And then . . .

A Mind of Their Own

Kaya dumped her backpack at the front door and headed for the kitchen, lured by the smell of brownies. "Mom, you're the greatest!" she said, as her mom pulled the pan from the oven.

"I know," her mom replied. "And that's not all. I got some shoes at a garage sale since you wrecked your old ones in that mud puddle incident."

"A garage sale?"

"Yes, that will have to do until we go shopping. Am I still the greatest?"

"I guess," said Kaya, biting into a warm brownie.

A few seconds later, she wiped her mouth and went to her room. Next to her bed sat odd-looking shoes, made of little colored squares sewn together with black thread. They were soft and lightweight, so she stuck her feet in them. Perfect!

"I'm going to Avery's house," she called, slamming the front door. But when she turned right at the sidewalk, she couldn't move. Her feet felt frozen to the cement. She strained to lift her legs, first one, then the other. It was useless. She couldn't move forward. She stared at her feet. *Those SHOES are doing this!* Her next impulse was to get home, and she was relieved to be able to turn around. She took a step, then another. *That's better.* But when she turned towards the front door, her feet, or those shoes, kept going straight. "Stop!" she yelled, but the shoes kept walking.

And then . . .

Stir the Soup

Ginny wanted to be a chef when she grew up. Today, she was practicing with soup. She started with a pot of broth and added some vegetables from the refrigerator, a few cans of this and that from the pantry, and several seasonings from the spice rack. She found some interesting-looking pasta shapes and tossed them in, too. Steam rose, and Ginny bent over the pot to sniff. It was okay, but nothing special. Time to see what the garden had to offer.

Ginny wandered through the beds, plucking leaves from this plant, bits from another, digging up a couple of strangely colored root vegetables. Then Ginny returned to the kitchen. She sliced and chopped and dumped all she had gathered into the pot.

Instantly the mixture hissed and sputtered. She stirred. She sniffed. It smelled . . . interesting. She took a sip, and jumped when it fizzed on her tongue. She stirred some more, round and round, watching the soup spin like a whirlpool. She let go of the spoon, but it kept circling the pot, round and round, all by itself. Grabbing hold of the spoon again, she tried to take it out of the pot. She couldn't. It yanked her arm in circles until she let go again. The spoon stopped, though the soup kept circling. It lifted itself out, scooped up some soup, and hung in midair. It came closer to her face, and Ginny knew what she was going to have to do. The spoon touched her lips. They opened, and she drank the soup.

And then . . .

A Pony for Your Thoughts

Emma stood at the mirror in her bathroom and wrestled with her ponytail. Her new pony binders were supposed to be "Magically Easy to Work With." So far, she wasn't impressed.

"Move over. I need the sink," her little sister muttered as she stumbled in sleepily.

"I'm almost done." Emma snapped the fat new pony binder in place.

"It looks stupid," Susie remarked.

"Excuse me?" Emma turned in surprise at her sister's rudeness.

"I didn't say anything."

"Yes you did. You said it looks stupid."

"I did not! I wouldn't say that!" Susie looked truly shocked.

Emma turned back to the mirror. She yanked the pony binder out of her hair, then tied it in again.

"I can think whatever I want, but I sure wouldn't say it out loud," Susie commented.

"Well then, why did you?" Emma demanded, yanking the band out a third time.

Cliffhanger Writing Prompts © 2011 by Teresa Klepinger, Scholastic Teaching Resources

"Why did I what?"

"Why did you say it out loud?"

Susie stared. "I didn't say anything out loud."

"You said 'I can think whatever I want, but I sure wouldn't say it out loud.'"

Susie's eyes grew round. "Emma, I thought that, but I didn't say it. I swear."

"I heard you plain as day." The two locked eyes as Emma slowly drew her hair back one more time and began to wind the rubber band around the ponytail. Just as it snapped into place, Emma heard her sister's voice.

"You're really freaking me out."

Only this time, Emma realized Susie's lips never moved.

And then . . .

Cliffhanger Writing Prompts © 2011 by Teresa Klepinger, Scholastic Teaching Resources

Lucky Day

Claire stood at the kitchen window and looked out to the pasture that used to be empty. "Mom! Our neighbors got a horse!" she yelled.

"Really? Grab an apple and go say hi," Mom called back.

In half a minute Claire was standing on the fence, the horse chewing the apple from her palm. *Hmmm. This horse looks REALLY old*, thought Claire. The horse was swaybacked and skinny, with a rough, scraggly coat and a lower lip that drooped and slobbered apple gunk on Claire's shoes. Her halter had a metal nameplate that said "Destiny." *Destiny, huh? That's quite a name for an old nag like you.*

Claire stepped down from the fence and was turning for home when Destiny tossed her head and stamped her hoof. "What's the matter with you?" Claire asked. Destiny stamped her front leg again and nosed the ground next to her hoof. Claire looked down and spotted a horseshoe. "Is this yours?" Destiny tossed her head a couple more times. Claire bent under the fence and grabbed the shoe. "Sorry you lost this. I'll tell Mom to let your owner know."

As she walked back to the house, she flipped the shoe around in her hands. An odd sensation prickled in her palms. She hooked the horseshoe in her back pocket and rubbed her hands on her jeans. That weird feeling went away. Once in her room, she left the horseshoe on her dresser and soon forgot about it.

The next morning when Claire woke up, she noticed the horseshoe. Curious, she picked it up and let it rest in her hands. There was no mistaking the tingly, buzzing feeling. Brief flashes of pictures flickered in her mind—her mom holding a basket of laundry, her cat with a mouse in its jaws, Aunt Bev standing at the door with her finger on the doorbell. Claire dropped the horseshoe and the pictures disappeared. *That was so creepy!* She headed to the kitchen for breakfast. Turning the corner into the room, she froze when she saw her cat outside the sliding glass door, chewing up the remains of a mouse.

"Honey," called her mom as she passed through the room with a laundry basket, "Make sure all your clothes are in the hamper. I'm doing laundry today."

Claire's hands trembled slightly as she reached for the TV remote and pressed the buttons for her favorite cartoon. Just as it blinked on, the doorbell rang. Her mom called, "There she is! Get dressed, sweetie, it's your aunt."

Claire gasped as she ran to her bedroom. *What does this mean?* She stared at the horseshoe. A moment later, she took a deep breath, picked up the horseshoe and grasped it firmly with both hands.

And then . . .

Cliffhanger Writing Prompts © 2011 by Teresa Klepinger, Scholastic Teaching Resources

On. Off. On. Off.

Carlos thought the present his brother gave him was okay, but that was the problem. It was just okay. It was a flashlight. What's so great about a flashlight? *I guess I can say it's mine and keep it in my room.* He'd wrap duct tape around the handle and put his name on it.

That night in bed, he got out his birthday present. *How lame. Why didn't he get me that pellet gun we talked about?* He switched it on and shone it at his closet. He could see his clothes hanging inside. *Oops, I forgot to shut my closet door. I hate that.* He got up to push the door closed, but was surprised to find it already shut tight. Confused, he climbed back in bed.

He aimed his flashlight at the ceiling and switched it on again. He saw cobwebs and beams of wood that made the roof of the house. Carlos shut the flashlight off. There was his ceiling, with glow-in-the-dark stars stuck to it. He switched it on again. Cobwebs, beams of wood, the roof. *Off.* Ceiling, stars. *On.* Cobwebs, beams, roof. *Off.* Ceiling, stars. *I get it. I can see through things.* He pointed it at the outside wall of his bedroom. There was the backyard, the swing set, the maple tree. *Off.* His wall, and a poster of Jump Shot Johnson.

A sneaky grin crossed Carlos's face. He climbed out of bed, and tiptoed out his bedroom door, flashlight in hand.

And then . . .

Notes